THE GENTLE ART

THE

GENTLE ART

poems

William Wenthe

LOUISIANA STATE UNIVERSITY PRESS ▌▌ BATON ROUGE

Published by Louisiana State University Press
lsupress.org

LSU Press Paperback Original

DESIGNER: Mandy McDonald Scallan
TYPEFACE: Minion Pro, text; Playfair, display

COVER ILLUSTRATION: *Nocturne: Blue and Silver—Cremorne Lights*, 1872,
James Abbott McNeill Whistler. Bequeathed by Arthur Studd, 1919. Photo:
Tate.

LIBRARY OF CONGRESS CATALOGING-IN-PUBLICATION DATA
Names: Wenthe, William, 1957– author.
Title: The gentle art : poems / William Wenthe.
Description: Baton Rouge : Louisiana State University Press, [2023] | "LSU
    Press Paperback Original."
Identifiers: LCCN 2023004048 (print) | LCCN 2023004049 (ebook) | ISBN
    978-0-8071-7871-3 (paperback) | ISBN 978-0-8071-8058-7 (pdf) | ISBN
    978-0-8071-8057-0 (epub)
Subjects: LCSH: Whistler, James McNeill, 1834–1903—Poetry. | LCGFT:
    Poetry.
Classification: LCC PS3573.E565 G46 2023 (print) | LCC PS3573.E565
    (ebook) | DDC 811/.54—dc23/eng/20230510
LC record available at https://lccn.loc.gov/2023004048
LC ebook record available at https://lccn.loc.gov/2023004049

for Daniel Raymund,

in "the likeliest place"

Oh, I would have done anything for my art.

—JAMES MCNEILL WHISTLER

CONTENTS

I.

Il peint, le maître Whistler,
Le mystère, le mist, l'air.
 —COMTE ROBERT DE MONTESQUIOU

Thames Music

Groan of hawser as barge heaves:
tide lipping the shingle shore,
ruffling below the bridge pier,

wavelets the dripping oar
bleeds into . . . as colors bleed . . .?
It is night, the river traffic moored,

and you sketch what you can,
of building, bridge, barge—
silhouettes in charcoal,

strokes: *suggestions.* As if
precomposing the lines of the staff
on which, come daylight, you'll trim

the notes of harmonized color. Reaching
for music, you called them "Nocturnes,"
after Chopin, who named a mood

on the keyboard for a time of night
that holds in abeyance
the thrum of day. And you:

can you paint
music—that crafting of sound
and silence, self-reflective

order "all art aspires to,"
as gin-slurred, sesquipedalian Swinburne
was prone to quote?

Today, in a hushed gallery
of the Tate, I'm sitting ten paces away
from *Nocturne: Blue and Silver—*

Cremorne Lights.
Twenty-two notes of gold
train a slow melody

of gas lamps on the shoreline, reflected
in counterpoint on the water.
But as I linger,

sky and river, their one
infusion of color, lift
out of the frame

and resonate—no, not music,
but what music shadows,
some great being, being quiet.

Domestic Nocturne

Tomorrow I fly east; my wife flies west.
Divided aims, a shared bed.
Wakeful with the prospect
of traveling, I hold a glass of wine
as she lies beside me,
releasing, sigh by sigh,
tensions our daughter tightly wound,
whose bedtime stories' last "The End"
fell like a final curtain on
the breathless run-on sentence of her day.

I study the nightfall in our room;
how darkness opens as my eyes adjust,
till it seems the room itself has tasted
what light there is, and savors it—
though it's me who takes it in:
the fog of painted wall, mass of bed
and bureau, dark starfish of ceiling fan.
Yellowish auras, behind window shade
and door, seem to frame the darkness—
like gold frames that Whistler made
(the painter I'm leaving home
to study) to frame his studies
of the coming-on of night.

I want to write this down, this poise,
this moment hung between two days,
this quiet quickening; but switching on the light
would spoil it, and roil my wife awake.
When it became too dark to paint
the London riverscape, Whistler learned
to memorize the scene, committing to his mind
the river's glow against the shapes of shadows
on the far bank, the pinprick gold of gaslights.

He could dedicate his memory
to his art. And yet found so forgettable
his own children—infants bundled
to orphanage, his grown son barely
acknowledged. How far, tomorrow,
my wife will travel to receive
an embryo—all we could do to conceive—
a composition of cells that carry within
a possible child. And again, the familiar pull
between the work I love (this expectant week
of haunting galleries), and love for my family.

But really, what choice? I love
both ways; so what if either
makes me long for the other? For now,
let me commit to memory
the gloom and glimmer of this room.
In my hand, the glass of wine collects
an ember of light I barely see, as I barely hear
my wife's breath, now a rhythm of rest.
Tomorrow, we travel. Tonight,
I'm more like my daughter, riding on
my waking, thrilled by this three-day-old, cheap,
bottom-of-the-bottle wine, as Art and Life—
the long and the short of it—bicker like gods
above the mythic vessel of our bed.

Portrait in Fragments

1852, 1881

In art class at West Point, one of Whistler's several
quirks of self-display (a cadet in poor standing)
is to ignore the human model as a whole,
and focus on rendering, say, a detailed hand.
Indifferent scholar: drawing's all he studies,
leaving history to generals, math to builders of trains.

Thirty years later, at an opening: he's trained
himself to record, without *looking*, the several
entrances of Society—duchess, diva, lord; to study
the pose of feigned surprise, the *bon mot;* to stand
among his pastels, and apart. The work of his hand
seen even in the room's decor: red, green, gold. A whole—

Maud's gown, too, ordered special. Maud, not yet wholly
recovered from laboring, by train, then ferry, then train,
to Paris. Tough crossing in winter, but her gloved hands
served to hide the absence of a ring. More than several,
the times she mentioned it to James, who would stand
for no talk of the matter, retreating to his studio.

At West Point, Whistler squints, studies
the lines of a shoulder, then concentrates whole-
heartedly on a foot. (Years later, his models will stand
—even patrons—like soldiers as they wait for him to train
colors on the palette: each hue of cloth, the several
shades of flesh, like tesserae, sorted beforehand.)

Glancing from model to page, with quickening hand
the cadet does eyes, knee, navel: as though a study
of body parts—another foot, an ear—random and several.
The pieces in place now, he pauses, that the whole
effect might be prepared for, while baffled classmates train
their eyes on his drawing, trying to understand.

Now Maud, away from the London scene, barely standing,
stops before the hospice door. She raises her hand,
hesitates, then rings. The virginal nuns are trained
in this agony of moan and sweat and blood. Maud studies
the paper, and signs it—signs away their child—a whole
life delivered up; from mother and father, severed.

Now several quick connecting strokes, and the figure stands
on paper, fully formed and whole, as if beneath his hand
any study from life could be easily trained.

Wig Lady

Every day but Sunday, we passed her and the wigs—
shelves and bins and spinning racks of wigs . . .

She worked out of the entryway to an empty
factory on 14th Street, whose landlords, desperate
for renters, would let a doorway to a wig seller,
and partition upper floors with sheetrock
and hack wiring into lofts, to rent illegally
to us—out of college and aspiring
painters, writers, dancers, a new wave band,
composers, architects—all hungry, all would-be:
all of us wanting to be received.

Every morning, heading for day jobs,
and returning every evening, day spent,
we ran that gauntlet of artificial hair
seeking to match every race and blend
of humanity. And further—fantastical, over-the-top
inventions: day-glo wigs in chartreuse, orange, rainbow;
red, white & blue wigs; fright wigs;
wigs for drag queens, clowns, and Halloween.

Saturday mornings, wandering out
to a late breakfast; or wandering in, head misty
from an all-night party, we'd find her there,
taciturn and stoic on her stool.
Two years I lived there, two years
nodding and smiling to her, yet now
it occurs to me: in two years I never saw
a customer. As we made our livings,
she made hers, purveying to longings
we could not imagine, owned by persons
we could not see, their needs as many and particular
as the God-numbered hairs on our heads.

Acknowledgments

Because I admired him,
years ago I shook the hand
of Allen Ginsberg, who
for similar reasons, years before,
shook the hand of Ezra Pound
who many decades earlier
had come to shake the hand
of William Butler Yeats. And he,
in the previous century, introduced
himself by shaking the hand
of Oscar Wilde who, aspiring,
had shaken the hand of James
McNeill Whistler who, removing
the monocle from his eye,
peered at the earnest young man,
initiating this centuries-spanning chain
of—what is the word? What is it
Marcel Proust was after, when he
purloined one of Whistler's gloves?

Tending: A Nocturne

They drank like I worked, in shifts. Saturday morning,
boilermakers for men coming off the nightshift at Nabisco. Midafternoon,
the martini guys, rewarding themselves for yard chores. A crew
before dinner; another crew after: all arriving at the Dutch House,
the tavern where, out of college, and trying to save myself
enough money for Europe, I served buck-fifty Manhattans,
vodka martinis, gimlets and kamikazes. Standard practice
was to fill the shaker near to the brim, wave the bottle of vermouth
in token salute, and hand them both shaker and glass.
How to tell the illness from the cure? They were workers, drinkers,
each in his way disturbed by a sense of something better;
or a hope: as if, the way a ten-dollar bill could transform into gin-
blossomed intoxication, so the shitty hand of twos and threes
they'd each been dealt might, if parleyed by imagination,
be bluffed into a flush or straight.
                                        Manhattan
rose on its pedestal, fifteen miles away; its pink corona
blazed against swampy summer nights, humid gauze
of my own thoughts, where there stayed, engraved in memory
by the mystery of their craft, images of disciplined perfection—
swells and spillings-over of the "Liebestod," or momentary hieroglyphs
of a Balanchine *pas de deux*—that could only belong, it felt like,
to *there*, where I'd seen them: not this suburban bar, or conveyor belt
at UPS where I loaded trucks on weekdays. I knew enough of irony to know
that I was like a Leonard Bast, gazing up at the groomed and decadent
Comte Robert de Montesquiou, in Whistler's portrait at the Frick—
if not for the irony that I'd never heard of either.
So, instead, this analogy, served straight: I kept those images
within me, the way the tiny shrines, dusty memorials
to some saint or grave event, are kept on gravel mountain roads in Greece,
tended and adored.

Between here and there, the commuter rail. Bergen county shortcut
of the former Erie Lackawanna. It crossed the Hackensack Meadowlands:
miles of reeds and backwaters, vast brackish tidal marsh
vectored by railroads and highways raised on piers; girdered
bridges, gantries, skeleton pylons of high tension lines;
the red-blinking towers of radio antennae, power-plant smokestacks.
Migrant ducks bobbing on the water, ink dots against sunset.
The white ascensions of scavenging gulls.

By ten o'clock, a weekend evening shift will have found
its mood. Maybe quiet, a little blue. Maybe tense—
one man's anger irritating us all. Or hilarious, like the night
when Channel 11 plugs a gap in programming caused
by an extra-inning Yankees game with *A Night at the Opera*,
and Harpo drops a sandbag on the arrogant tenor,
and Groucho and Chico each place a foot upon
his cold-cocked, coattailed torso, like a human bar rail;
and Groucho says, "Two beers, bartender," to which Chico chimes,
"I'll have two beers, too." And for an evening, it seems the angel
of comedy has dropped in, and is buying rounds for us all.
Most nights, though, eleven o'clock arrives mellow, forgettable;
except I'm waiting for the punctual thrill
of Wayne, the painter's, arrival.

I never saw his paintings, but I knew his habits:
weekends or covering a weeknight shift, I'd anticipate
the rush of the door, and Wayne's entrance, ebullient or moody,
usually with a bit of bluster, thirsty for talk and Budweiser.
He worked his day job by day; and each night, like punching
a time clock, he painted in his basement studio.
Wayne gave me evidence—my first—of what it meant,
in a day-in, day-out sense, to be a working artist. I mean,
he worked a job, he worked his art. What I don't mean

is that his art made him a living. Sure, I'd seen others' works—
staged, hung in a gallery, set on a page—but not till Wayne
had I seen the guy coming in after a session
where maybe everything went wrong, to shrug it off
and talk: our gin mill in north Jersey his *Lapin Agile,*
his *Café du Dome,* his Cedar Tavern. The other thing he gave me
was credit. He committed to memory a line I'd written,
one of the few to survive that time; he let it enter his pantheon
of things worth repeating and discussing, each night
as if for the first time. A leitmotif, along with "Wind and Window Flower,"
and Scotland, and McEwan's Ale, and Whistler's *Gentle Art
of Making Enemies,* and above all, Whistler's art.

Whaddya wanna go to Greece for? one of the regulars asks,
after I'd told him my plans. *Ya got all the Greeks ya want
down the Empress Diner.* I thought of Whistler, same age as me,
carrying two hats as he walks to work at the Coastal Survey.
(The stories Wayne told me, quickening in my thoughts.)
One to hang on the hat rack at work, the other to wear
to a nearby tavern, where he'd shoot pool and sketch the locals.
Once for a routine rendering of a harbor entrance,
he drew two boys fishing from a bridge—human figures
to give a human scale, as in the engravings he'd seen
of ancient ruins. *Get rid of them,* his supervisor snapped.
So he places them on the bank. Again: *Get rid of them.*
The next version: two small tombstones at water's edge.
So why not, soon as he gets a little money,
quit that job he was bound to lose anyway, and sail to France?

Once and once only, in a gray suit I boarded
the 8:15 train to the city, to look for jobs. A morass
of faces, protective of their seats, deflected mine
in the crowded car that could have been the ferry

of forgetful dead. My puny claim to almost nothing
forbade me to judge them except by the gut reaction:
I cannot live like you. This was my spleen talking,
my bowels, my bones. I'd not yet heard the phrase,
Épater la bourgeoisie, but believe me, that day,
the bourgeoisie épatéed the shit out of me.

More often I'd ride the same line in the afternoon,
the near-empty coach passing weathered hides
of shut down factories, then cross the Meadowlands,
in late winter light turning brass. At Hoboken terminal,
I'd descend the stairs to the PATH train beneath the river.
Sometimes, meeting at dusk the outbound commuters,
I'd slip behind the station to the piers, and the expanse
of the Hudson, and the water-given view of Manhattan—
floating, made simple (Where the homeless? Where
the limousines?), crystallized by distance. One could say, *composed.*
But I had nothing to say, dumb as any barnacle clung
to pilings of docks. Even so, I knew enough
to be silenced at the twilight blending of a city on a river.
As Wordsworth once, and Whistler, and on this same water—
half river, half harbor—Whitman and Crane.

Mid-March, early spring in North Jersey. We have little to say—
Frank, the owner, and I, having a nightcap
after my last night at the bar. In two days I fly to Athens.
Soon I will come to pause, at the dusty cabinet of a shrine
by a mountain road in Crete. By summer I'll walk along the Thames,
in long northern twilight—when twilight still had a chance
(the waterfront today lit up like a birthday cake);
when coal was still unloaded for the looming, Doric stacks
of Battersea power station, massive enough to swallow cathedrals,
and garbage barges departed from the Grosvenor Canal.
But nothing to say about that, tonight. It had yet to happen.
Tonight is a lull. All Greece and England: potential. Tensed

in this moment like the wound spring of DNA, poised to coil
the past into the future; that future mirrored now in memory.
Wherein: I step from the Thames bank to Tate Museum, and eye
my first *Nocturnes*—moments, Whistler wrote, "When the whole city
hangs in the heavens." Here is slag heap and barge, bridge
and factory; gaslight, and the tidal river reflecting it, and taking
the *heavens,* which is only a painted word for *sky,* into its surface,
like pigment on a canvas, like a vision of Ascension, here realized.
I do not look at them; I drink. I partake.
I have toiled hard, and I am thirsty.

II.

Be warned in time, James; and remain, as I do, incomprehensible . . .

—OSCAR WILDE

The Artist Is Born in Lowell

When the critic, conditioned by his time
as any Galápagos finch by its island,
laid eyes on Whistler's *Nocturne in Grey*
and Gold: Chelsea Snow, he fell in love
with the small dark figure of a man
lonesome against the glow of lamplit windows
in the snow that "signifies life's tribulation."

Whistler seethed: *Who am I—Dickens?*
—A sin against art, to admit any motive
but the painting's own, which requires,
right there, that man-shaped wisp of black.
And Whistler's right—just hold up a thumb
to cover that figure, that single note, and see
the entire composition fizzle flat.

But even so, how can I resist
the temptation to snoop for motives?
Maybe that walking shadow of a man
is on a quest to his local pub
for the grail of a pint. And then
there's the question of original sin:
to picture Whistler himself,

the four-year-old boy, hidden beneath
his mother's dressing table, sketching her
over and over, as if his grip
on the pencil could draw him closer.
Two younger brothers will die
by the time he turns nine. At fifteen,
when his father dies, he'll decide

to become a painter. Years later the mother
describes her grown son, painting, rubbing out,
painting over, "until his genius is satisfied."
And yes, I can see the genius
played by that one black note.
But I can also feel the pressure of
a hand—just there—to satisfy

a need for focus in a scene dissolving
into formless mist and snow. I see
the hand of a young boy become the hand
of an old man who, asked in jest
"Whatever possessed you to be born
in *Lowell?*" replied, as if it had been scripted,
"I wanted to be near my mother."

Annie Seated

etching by Whistler

The gallery sign calls it "revery," but it's injustice,
you can tell, she's brooding on: adults
who force her to sit, in starched dress, still,
like a doll left on a chair.
Her sleeves are itchy; Uncle most fussy, scratching
onto metal plate her all-encompassing
pout. Head bowed, hair hanging
like a veil, shoulders
sloped: all frame her downcast
eyes, her pursed lips. She stares
at her hands in her lap; the left clasps
the right like a wounded bird. Her mood
is echoed by the shadow cast
by drooping head—a mood her uncle,
twenty-four and already etching like Rembrandt,
captures and inflicts by his art.

Whistler Paints a Portrait

Working by daylight,
this painter, in striped trousers,
patent leather, weskit of yellow silk,
gleaming collar and cuffs ("Costume,"
said Wilde, "is character without
description") glides from palette table
to canvas, with long-handled brush
touching paint from palette
to picture: a butterfly
sipping nectar, spreading pollen.

But the simile chosen by witnesses
of the crafty performance
(portrait sitter, studio visitor) is more
pointed—the advance, lunge, retreat
of the duelist; the long, foibled,
blade of brush the sword
in this *phrase d'armes*
of colors. "Drawing the life
right out of me," protested
Montesquiou, who became
Arrangement in Black and Gold.

Often as not, the day's work
wiped out with spirits and rag,
until some impasse between
two visions standing before him—
the living person (*Damn you!*
he screams, *Don't move!*)
and the composition
fashioned on canvas—is broken.
And the last stroke, or strike,
the *coup de grace*: his signature,
stylized butterfly.

The Chelsea Girl

"The sketch of an afternoon,"
wrote Whistler, which is still more time
than any gentleman would pay
to a costermonger girl—
unschooled, gutter-mouthed urchin
orbiting like a comet from the family
fruit barrow, screaming up a sale—
bugle-voiced and fearless.

In the center of the Empire,
she lives on the edge of it,
accosting the fine-cloaked
Londoners, cheekiness gauged
to the length of the leash
of the law—constables she'll dress
down in words as choice
as any rotten, heirloom
apple flung at its mark.

In Whistler's portrait, she stands
feet apart, hands braced on hips,
a stout A, like Henry VIII
in Holbein's portrait, except,
being small, she is looking *up.*
A yellow "kingsman" round her neck
(the fruit seller's trademark scarf),
a hand-me-down man's floppy hat:

these frame what the painter spent
the best of his attention on:
the set of a young jaw edged
by shadow, pursed lips and russet round
of cheeks, wide brown eyes,
and the raised arch—
What you think YOU'RE looking at?—
of the eyebrows. Who knows

what Whistler paid her
for *her* time. He gave away
this painting to pay off
a private debt, and she remains
(according to the catalog
where I admire her greatly
diminished reproduction)
even now, in a private collection,
still standing like a king.

Two Lonelinesses

In a traffic lull on King's Road I catch myself
singing an old song. And I remember,
traveling years ago, an isolation so raw
my only comfort was the song I shaped
with my breath. This time, I've come
to glean what faintest traces might remain
of a painter who died a few streets from here
a hundred years ago. Torn down,
bombed, rebuilt, many times paved over:
London's metamorphosed even since,
near thirty years ago, in a hushed gallery,
I first saw the riverine, dusk,
and distant gas-lamp glow of his *Nocturnes.*

Back then I traveled for traveling's sake,
as if traveling were an engine
I could open the throttle on, moving faster
toward whatever comes. Now the ache
has focus: I strain to picture my daughter,
as if, by heart pulse and synapse and prayer,
I could hold her. And too, this release—
temporary—from the troubles
with my wife: all the worked-for life
I am *away from.* How thrilling

and banal, to be alone, walking now
past townhouses, and glimpses windows afford
of dining tables, bookshelves, lamps,
paintings on the walls: harmonized interiors
not my own. And questioning whether
to resist or indulge the reflex urge to sing.

Rotherhithe

Only that underlying sense
Of the look of a room on returning thence.
—THOMAS HARDY

I.

Downstream of Tower Bridge, where Bermondsey Wall overlooks
a reach of lacquered mud low tide reveals,
I stop to watch some dozen people with buckets and brooms.
They tend a row of nine squared timbers
laid flat, half-sunk, half-risen
in mud, and a larger timber, curved on one side like a rudder.
I don't know why they're here—the timbers,
the people. Only, that the picture
of these persons brushing, sweeping, heads bowed
in simple labor, appears like a peasant scene,
a harvest scene. And in the manner of so many paintings,
some of them stand, observing, as if to be of a company
with you, the observer, peering through the frame. Or me,
in this case, who can walk down a stone stairway,
and step into the scene, and ask.

II.

Seated at a table in the Angel Inn,
I thought back to the strange, tide-hidden,
carefully spaced rank of wooden beams, and the persons
attending them. Something about their attention—ritual
and casual at once (porkpie hats, billed caps, Wellies)—
Brueghel could have painted them, in the clothing of his day.
Or the Limbourg brothers, for the medieval book of hours.
Ritual: I mean what Pound said of rhythm—
a shape cut in time. A present that is also past;
and vice versa, to turn the times, like the tide, around.

III.

A pint of Sam Smith's Extra Stout
in the early afternoon: another sort of ritual,
pints in a pub. This my second—during the first
I explored this pub that's been pouring beer
since before Victoria took the throne:
the front room and bar, the back parlor,
and the smaller parlor to its right—and various
nooks, bays, hearths; then the balcony, overlooking
the tide, and the stairs where rivermen
would enter from skiffs, for a quick lift of whiskey,
or for bed and board. Rogues, tars, bilge-rats,
and at least one painter, all here at the Angel,
a meeting place between river and land.

IV.

And in fact, it was a ship's rudder,
the man told me, in the tide-mud meeting place
between river and land. A sailing vessel
from the eighteenth century, dismantled; its timbers
and rudder laid down as skids for a drydock.

Old beams disused, seen anew, re-used:
seated at a table at the Angel Inn, I'm all
cleverness now, afloat on ale:
thoughts slide in, catch the tide, set sail:
the membered past, scrounged and rejiggered, passes on . . .

in relics of beams and rudder
that once bore a crew, cargo, and a name,
a carved and painted figure on the bowsprit;
to become in time a static staging ground,
threshold of other ships' sailing forth.

Or as metamorphosis: I'm looking at this pub again,
rebuilt and refurbished—like a human body, cell
by cell; a rotten rafter here, cracked plank there, nails
winter-loosened. Whale-oil lanterns replaced
by gas lamps, then wired for electricity.

V.

What is it they're after? The assiduous crew
of volunteers hauls Thames water in buckets,
"cleaning what can be seen," they tell me.
How the mud-sunk rudder steers them, still,
toward some aura, like a saint's bone, a power

not of force, but connection. *Aura,*
as Benjamin described the pull
of a work of art, that thrill—to be in its presence—
impossible to reproduce.
                              I'm staring now
at a cheap framed print of Whistler's painting,
Wapping, on the wall of the Angel Inn.
And I'm sitting almost exactly where the painter sat
while painting it. The presence that I'm after
is not so much a thing to see,
but something *seen.*
                        Across the water,
the warehouses rise, with old names: Phoenix
Wharf, St. John's Warehouse, King Henry's Wharf.
They're luxury flats now; their prior functions marketed
as charm. The boats are fewer, sleeker now:
police boats and party boats, all waiting
for different events.
                        Gone, the webwork
of masts and spars and rigging that had so caught
his eye. And yet, even now, the feel of the balcony—the frame
that grounds and gives onto the scene—
is eerily the same . . .

VI.

                 . . . but gone:
those three figures on the balcony.
The two men conspiring, leaning in over the table.
The woman, leaning back, gazing out
of the picture, into the Inn. Or nowhere.
Her eyes are fixed, like a carved figure on a bowsprit.
We know her name: she is Jo Heffernan,
Whistler's mistress. The man next to her, Alphonse Legros,
a painter friend he knows from Paris. Whistler spent years
getting their faces right, to render their expressions
as though they are *here,* in this moment
the painting presents as the present. Only now,
in the here of the Angel Inn,
where it almost seems I step into the scene,
it is their absence that haunts the balcony.
And the absence has a feel.
                 —But how to say this
in words, except by words' own contradictions? I say
the *actual* absence of those now gone, who hewed
that rudder; who steered, rode that vessel:
the tangible evidence of absence.

VII.

Three figures seated at a table. I see
three old-timers at the Angel Inn, nursing
their pints, telling stories of boats
they've bought and sold: their past dealings
dealt again through telling—
th' fuckin' boat I fuckin' bought off Bobby . . .
We come for the past but not the past alone.
We know no past alone,
only what of it we encounter
now: we come to find that bearing
of past on present, and vice versa, to turn

the times, like the tide, around—history and
my living body—*my fuckin' body*—
confused: the liminal place. Meaning *threshold*.
Meaning window, balcony. Tidal river. Frame.

III.

Where is the time, my friend, where we were happy,
with no concerns but those of art . . .

    —GUSTAVE COURBET

Letter to Whistler

Stéphane Mallarmé

Not the ruffled, irrelevant gusts
such as occupy the streets
subject to the dark flight of hats,
but a dancer appearing

in whirlwind of muslin or fury
scattered into spindrift
she uplifts with her knee—
this same she for whom we lived—

in order to blast with the tutu
all, apart from him, that's hackneyed,
droll, drunken, sluggish,
with no other hint of rancor

than laughter that puffs the air
of her skirt to fan Whistler.

The Artist Is Reborn

> The time has gone by when a man shall be born
> without being consulted!
> —WHISTLER

*James Abbott McNeill Whistler was born on July 10, 1834, at
Lowell, Massachusetts, in the United States of America.*

So your first biography begins. And were it possible
that we could meet, I might begin along similar lines,

like another American who, spying your signature
appearance in the lobby of the Carlton, said:

> "*You know, Mr. Whistler, we were both born at Lowell, and at
> very much the same time. There is only the difference of a year—
> you are sixty-seven and I am sixty-eight.*"

You know, a little small talk. Find some common ground.
Ain't that American? But I'd have to reckon

a lot of babies arrived in Lowell that year.
It's not as if you sauntered out of the womb

with top hat, monocle, weskit, and walking stick;
or that young woman, your mother, had already become

the aged widow, arranged and painted, purchased
by the French, where she hangs in the Musée d'Orsay.

Nope. Something happened along the way. A metamorphosis:
but more than the numb compulsion of caterpillar

to butterfly; rather, an assertion, with a flourish,
like the butterfly—with stinger—by which you sign your letters;

or the way you squeezed the history of culture
into a single lecture, presented at ten o'clock of a Friday,

so that the refined would have time to dine. . . . Something akin
to your style, which begged and defied caricature: "Quite too

Utterly Utter," the title of a music hall song
that granted your fashion the homage of mockery.

For after all, any fool can be born. No talent in that;
no Selection Committee to pass through for membership

in the populace. Why, popularity, to you, was a painter's
perdition. And so, to the fellow American extending his hand:

> *"Sir, I do not choose to be born at Lowell, and I refuse*
> *to be sixty-seven."*

The Trial

James McNeill Whistler, Plaintiff,
v. John Ruskin, Defendant

Twenty-three, one year out of college,
The first time I saw the *Nocturnes* of Whistler.
As I approached to pay them homage,
I leaned in close, and then still closer.
This, to the gallery guard, was sacrilege:
"Keep one foot away, please," he hissed, "*Sir.*"
So as a sort of gag, and not unkindly,
I stuck one foot straight out behind me.

A defensive gesture, a little vaudeville—
Showing that, for critical intelligence,
I barely had a leg to stand on. My school
Was impulse: on one hand, irreverence,
And on the other, a solemn urge to kneel.
To speak of it now, much older, I need a stance
That straddles serious and ironic:
Ottava rima—both Yeatsian and Byronic.

So thirty years on, I'm back at the Tate,
Before his *Nocturne: Blue and Gold—Old Battersea
Bridge.* Standing back, I contemplate
How light of sky and water seem to free
Themselves from darkened bridge piers, elevate
Beyond the canvas, as well as gather me
Inside it. If paint were soul, then this would be,
In twilight shades of blue, an ecstasy.

"But which part is the bridge?" said Baron Huddleston,
Presiding in the Royal Court of Justice.
He's holding the same *Nocturne* upside-down.
(They'd passed it round the courtroom, just as

Though it were a flask; in passing rattled one
Poor chap's cranium, jarring frame from canvas.)
The Judge's question is more a riddle than complaint:
He couldn't tell the painting from the paint.

This was the trial of Whistler versus Ruskin.
Whistler wanted Ruskin in the dock—
To face the Oxford don, unmask him;
Expose him, like a shilling Vermeer, as fake.
Whistler's challenge was at best a risky one;
His wealth (of mortgages and debts) at stake.
But Ruskin would avoid the public takedown,
Pleading "illness" to cover a nervous breakdown.

It had the makings of an operetta
(W. S. Gilbert was in the audience,
Perhaps imagining a new libretto).
But underneath the matinee performance
Was motive for a genuine vendetta:
The Artist would expose the Critic's fraudulence,
And prove that paintings need not bear at all
On meanings legal, moral, ethical.

The libel had its birth in Ruskin's fury
At *Nocturne in Black and Gold*, at such disgrace
(He wrote) *To hear a coxcomb ask two hundred guineas*
For flinging a pot of paint in the public's face.
Well, that, and *ill-educated* and *Cockney*
impudence. Oh, and *wilful imposture.* Still, the case
For the Defense was simple: one cannot sue
If they can prove what Ruskin said is true.

And for the job: Attorney General,
Queen's Counsel, MP, one Sir John Holker.
Yet more than rank and title, his best credential
Is common sense, for he's a straight talker,

And gives no slack to intellectual
Humbug; knows hawk from handsaw, piss from nectar.
All in a day's work. But enjoy it much? He can't have—
For truth be told, he rather liked the plaintiff.

But let the degradation start. A question:
"Isn't that a stiffish price, to those
Of us who aren't artists?" Cross-examined,
Whistler, monocled, affects a candid pose,
Responds with "Very likely so." The hint taken,
The audience chortles sportingly—it knows
The joke's on them. After they've had their laugh:
"The picture: how quickly did you knock it off?"

"I beg your pardon?" Then Sir John, amicable,
Showing he too can play the Joker:
"It's an expression, I'm sure, more applicable
To my own profession." Then Whistler: "As for *knocking
It off*—(and thank you for the compliment)—a couple
Of days is ample time." And Holker:
"The work of two days . . ." (he braces for the *finis*),
"And for *that* you dare to ask two hundred guineas?"

"No," says Whistler. And then a resonant pause.
"I ask it for the knowledge I have gained
In the work of a lifetime." Thunderous applause.
Judge Huddleston, as if to keep his brain
From exploding, grabs his powdered wig, & gavels
The court to silence. "I shall make myself plain:
This is no theatre, I am no D'Oyly Carte.
Applaud once more and I will clear the court."

—Ah, Your Lordship! Along with justice, you must
Balance gravity and levity
In the scales. But how on earth can you resist
A joke? To *not* say, with mock authority,

"It is the painting, not Mr. Irving, I trust,
That is the 'Arrangement in Black'"? Felicity
insists that you should quip, of Joseph Mallord
William Turner's *Snow Storm*—"Lobster salad."

But isn't this the problem: how to speak
Of art? "Of course, it's a matter of *taste*,"
Says one, defending Ruskin's right to critique.
"And of course, you're wrong," jabs Whistler in riposte;
"It isn't taste, it's knowledge." To know technique,
He says, to practice craft, makes a judgment just:
If expertise derived from merely looking on,
The museum guard's as good any don.

And painting, like math, must make internal sense,
Equations not of numbers, but of paint.
But *Nocturnes* have "no moral elements,"
His critics testify. And so the campaign
Now mounted by Sir John for the Defense:
To batter Whistler's *Battersea Bridge,* and taint
The painting with sarcastic niggling;
And while he's at it, keep the courtroom giggling.

"Is this a fire escape, or a telescope?
Why not draw a bridge that seems a bridge?
And what about these figures on the top—
Are they people? Cattle? Horse and carriage?
How'd they come to be there? *How* do they hope
To come down? This darkling smudge is what, a barge?
And why has blue paint wandered onto the frame?
Such work, shown publicly, invites a public shame."

"I think that I should call it 'Originality,'"
Says a Whistler witness to Holker's harangue.
The lawyer would impose the personality
Of the painter on the paintings, and thereby hang

The painter by his pictures. The quality
Of mercy won't be strained when time to bring
The painting that caused it all, and attack it:
Nocturne in Black and Gold: The Falling Rocket.

Now, with Whistler in the witness box,
Sir John Holker, Member of Parliament,
Attorney to the Queen, assumes his mask
Of ordinary chap, no different
Than the "gentlemen of the jury," and deigns to ask:
"Do you think that you yourself—having spent
Your lifetime in this business—can, if you please,
Make me see the beauty of this piece?"

In *The Gentle Art of Making Enemies,*
Whistler lingers on this telling juncture—
He waits, "examining attentively"
The lawyer's countenance, and then the picture;
Regarding one, and now the other, as patiently
The court in silence waits to hear the answer:
"No! It would be quite as hopeless, I fear,
As music to a man who cannot hear."

By now, the lawyer knows he can't prevail
Against the painter with aesthetic taunts.
So he'll conjure for the jury what he'll call
"Artistic Ladies" as the audience
For Whistler's *Nocturnes*—swooning, hysterical:
The critic's role displaced by sycophants.
His point: society shall fall apart
If women are the arbiters of art.

Now even Whistler's lawyer, Sergeant Parry,
As eminent a Victorian as can be, is shocked.
"What of women artists?" he asks the jury:
"And shall their excellence be overlooked?"

His question, in part, is a ploy most lawyerly;
And yet, defending one who has been mocked
By men in power, it holds a kind of mirror
Of equality before the face of every juror.

This notion the jury brought into sequester
Along with this and that and the other thing
Mentioned by Huddleston, whom they pestered
With questions and with quarreling
Before delivering their ambivalent answer:
Verdict for the Plaintiff; Damages: one farthing.
Whistler declared the trial a victory,
Although, for lawyer's fees, he'll file for bankruptcy.

"Naughty Critic . . . Silly Painter!" says the cartoon
In *Punch,* sparing neither adversary.
So easy for cartoonists to lampoon
A love of art. Another one, exemplary:
The newly married, tasteful couple croon
Among displays of fine chinoiserie:
Holding up a most exquisite teapot,
One says, "Dear Love, let us live up to it."

So just how serious is our stake in art?
Gilbert and Sullivan made fun of Oscar Wilde,
And Whistler himself was featured in a farce;
In our time, Mr. Bean sneezed and soiled
The famous *Whistler's Mother,* and drew a car-
Toon face on her, banana-nosed and bald.
But then the news: cartoonists murdered at *Charlie
Hebdo;* and, for writing poetry,

A girl gets beaten in an Afghan town,
Her crime the worse because she spoke of love.
And yet the chaste and pious Taliban
Pleasure themselves with poems reeking of

Sentimental crap for martyrdom's renown:
McGonagall carrying a Kalashnikov.
Is art idolatry? Or art the temple?
Is it "to die for"? The answer isn't simple.

As for the *Nocturne in Black and Gold,*
It's in Detroit, at the Institute of Arts.
For fourteen years it would remain unsold,
Dimmed, perhaps, by the shadow of the courts.
And when it sold, it fetched a handsome, cold
Eight hundred guineas, which felt like just deserts
For Whistler, who, with gentle unrestraint,
Said "Go tell Ruskin—*four* pots of paint!"

Sonnet

Next time you're visiting a gallery, linger
A moment on the space between the paintings.
The old Salons would hang them floor to ceiling,
Side to side, covering the walls like shingles.
Hence those frames—gilded, bulky props
Meant not only to enclose, but for keeping out
The other crowded works and their competing shouts
For attention like ads, pop-ups, or apps.

It was Whistler's thought, to give the paintings space.
If you've never paid attention to the walls,
That's the point: to give the eye a pause,
Some room to let the painting, as you see it,
Resonate. Like silence after a musical phrase,
Or, as he wrote, "the large margins framing the sonnet."

Bankrupt

1866, 1879

I.

Early in the outbound voyage, turning
toward twilight, three ships westering
in the strait between the mainland and Wight.
(A ghostly fourth, liminal on misted horizon)

The painting is called a *Nocturne* but only
after the fact. A *maritime,* Whistler might have called
these ships at sea. Soothing brush-waves of blue and green,
roseate undertones; suffused in communion of sea and sky,
where ships seem not so much to float, as fly;
or no, not the ships, but the eye—
this is art. It seems a gift, this painting
that came to him as though a bird, crossing
the water, had alighted on his canvas to rest:
this vision he'd spend years
trying to attain again.

II.

Between Bohemia and the *haute bourgeoisie,*
he had flitted like a butterfly
while Americans fought their Civil War. His brother,
a Confederate doctor, had spent the war
sawing off legs sausaged by cannon.
Whistler himself had served under General Lee—
as a West Point cadet, that is—before he failed
his chemistry exam for the final time.
"Had silicon been a gas," goes the joke he told,
"I'd be a Colonel by now." Soldier, gentleman,
and Southerner—or so he fancied himself, his mother
the daughter of a Carolina planter. But why,
in 1866, he suddenly wrote his will
and sailed to Valparaíso, he never gave a cause.

A war there, of sorts: the Spanish fleet,
being comprised of gentlemen, announced
the day and the appointed hour
for a morning's bombardment from the harbor.
Whistler fled on horseback—along with *the whole
fraternity speaking the English language*—to watch
from the outlying hills. *And then I knew
what a panic was,* he wrote. Hours later,
riding back to town, they were set upon
by little children in the streets, mocking them.

His only real combat didn't come
until returning home to London. *He offended
my prejudices as a Southerner,* wrote Whistler,
of a Haitian on board, of richly dark complexion.
His offense: being seated as an equal at the table.
Whistler, waiting on deck, grants himself the right
to cock his foot and kick the *black scoundrel.*
The Haitian—military, proud, and certainly
nobody's slave, least of all this shrill
American who calls him *Captain Marmalade,*
returns with a sword, and proceeds
to slap Whistler with the flat of the blade
until he's bored with slapping.

III.

As to *these unseemly discussions
about the bill,* writes Whistler to the grocer
who has declined the offer of two Nocturnes
in recompense, *most excellent people*
have dined on these tomatoes and fruit:
a splendid advertisement. He encloses the bill,
unpaid. It is 1879, and his house is now for sale;

bailiffs lounging about the lower floor,
posted there to protect—from Whistler—
his furniture tagged and numbered for auction.
Still, appearances must be kept up, a certain
position maintained. Tonight he entertains
a prospective buyer for his paintings. Eighteen pence,
borrowed from a chum, buys three bottles of *vin ordinaire*
and sealing wax, in three colors, which he uses
to seal the corks, as though some vintage worthy
of decades' keeping. The bailiffs, charmed
by Whistler, wait at table. "Bring to me
the bottle with the yellow seal," he commands,
to commence the meal. Between soup and cutlets,
"Bring the bottle with the blue seal." With cheese
and walnuts, "the bottle with the red seal."

Diary: — Nov. '79. Dined last night at Whistler's. Attending were Wm. Ros-
setti, Sir and Lady ——— .Whistler in high spirits; admire his resolution in
wake of trial and financial ruin. Eager, then, to show me his work. The por-
trait of Carlyle, seated sideways, eyes fixed on some far-off moral—spurn-
ing our company, it would seem. *Nocturnes*—and the one lately contested
in his lawsuit. *Black and Gold*—striking, for what it's worth—although, now
I think about it, the question of its worth *was* the crux of the trial. Silently
I toyed with the notion of buying it. He goaded me: "Who purchases this, I
assure you, inscribes his name in the annals of art, and the right side of his-
tory." I said, "I should think posterity rightly belongs to the artist, not the
buyer." Though I dare say, the opposite may well be true: that it is Whistler's
personality has made the painting famous. (As mere monetary investment
it is worth consideration. Perhaps if my name can be kept out of it.)

Over dinner we discussed the ownership of art—more like a steward-
ship, a trust. As though art were an estate: a landscape akin to land, in
that it shall outlive the owner. I, a man of business, espy his calculation:
inferring that a man of wealth like myself, but of no landed estate, might
find such a legacy in art. Whistler as shrewd a salesman as artist. A higher
class of costermonger, he, but without the cursing.

As to the supper itself: it was rather like a child's tea party, all pretend: attentive in detail—a menu in French—but then, the bailiffs waiting table! And yet, how they threw their hearts into the performance, these rude mechanicals; these layabouts: Cinderella's lizards, transformed—how does he do it?—into footmen.

And yet: his discussion of stewardship—how winningly he frames it. Did he not recognize how my earlier comment (that I'd rather fame befall the artist) had prepared the ground? I have to admit a certain—affinity— for him. Did he see this affinity there, already; or did he create it? His personality is like fine wine: at first, one discriminates complexities of taste . . . meanwhile, the alcohol, having no taste at all, works you the same as any swill. Warms you to affection, or disputation; to being a friend, or enemy.

And so for the wine: such priestly procedurals! The decantation; then swirl and sniff and sip; the pompous pouring. But the wine itself, each bottle, was always the same. Could I discern any difference among them, 'twould be a miracle worthy of the young Christ Himself!

If only an evening could be orchestrated. . . .
Or, like a painting-in-progress, wiped down
and tried again. If only—if only—I could join
the dinner hosted by Whistler in 1879.
Propped there, adjacent the dining room,
paintings I've traveled far as Tulsa and Paris to behold;
as the man who crafted them conducts
his audience, until the painter, buoyant
with wine and witticism, launches
on the story of his voyage to Valparaíso.

In his telling, Whistler has booted this "Captain
Marmalade" across the deck to the top of a stairs,
whereupon, a lady ascending, he elevates
his hat, allows her to pass, then undertakes
to boot the man down the stairs. For always,
there is a rising and descending, a placing
of one above, the other below. In the story,

an order enforced: the de facto brig
of his cabin, where Whistler is confined
by command, under posted guard, becomes,
in the raconteur's recounting, a place of privilege,
where he enjoys—"an unusual courtesy"—
the "full permission to smoke." A most exclusive
company of one.
                    And yet his guests seem less
than dazzled. Crumbs, dregs, a wound of wine
on white linen. The famous smile. A peal
of that famous laugh, his last attempt to make the sale.

IV.

In a gallery, just down the lawn from the white
rondure and columned harmony
of the Capitol, I am trying to gauge my dislike
for Whistler's *Nocturne in Blue and Gold: Valparaiso Bay.*

An ugly, blockish pier; a confused
Crowd milling there, ill-painted, in a slurry
of dark smudge and swirl. More like a stain,
an intention he would take back. Some ships
at a distance, one in full sail, the others furled
and anchored. So, why these people on the pier?

There is no ship to take them anywhere.
It's as if he doesn't know what to do with them.
As if, trying to find his way to that vision
that visited him on the voyage out, the purposes
of people get reduced to a problem
of artistic composition
he cannot solve.

Even the heavy gilt frame,
as if to compensate, takes up more space
than the painting itself, which Whistler once tried
to trade to a grocer to settle a bill.

The City

I think of Cavafy's indelible poem,
and the phrase, as rendered by Durrell:
no ship exists to take you from yourself.
Thus Whistler, after his yearlong sail
to Valparaíso, stepping off the train
at Paddington Station, is met by a man
who promptly beats the shit out of him.

Living in a Masterpiece

the old Grosvenor Canal, London

For hours inside the Tate, the *Nocturnes*
of Whistler hushed me in their gold and charcoal,
blue-greens, grays. Outside, sun has burned

the mist away, and blares with dazzling overkill—
just the sort of light that gave him doubt,
flattering the fustian surface detail

coddled by painters he couldn't live without
despising. I walk between the river,
low-tide quiet, and Grosvenor Road, rush-hour loud,

and come to a bankside wedge of land, recovered
by grasses, shrubs, a velarium of trees.
A heron on a piling gives a sort of shiver,

then settles for a nap. And here are bees,
a jackdaw, spiderwebs, flowers gone to seed;
and blackbird song, above the traffic noise.

An accidental refuge (it's not like we can read
such places on a map) where a pair of moorhens
swim into a tunnel that leads

beneath the street—to a teacup tidal basin
below Victorian gates of a canal.
Above its tide-stained, mossy margins,

new buildings angle upward, chic and minimal.
Still, they've kept the old machinery
of locks, with railings, mitered gates, and wheels.

It beckons toward the nineteenth century . . .
that iron swing bridge an iron corridor
transporting me into a retro revery

where maybe Whistler, riding down Grosvenor,
might have seen these workings, might have worked
them in a *Nocturne*—if closer to the water.

Now, they're merely iron artifacts—
signifiers of an old mechanical order;
above them, sleek and glassy flats project

an avant-garde frisson, postmodern cool
I'll never have the income to afford.
But now I shudder at something weird:

the canal leads on to a reflecting pool
rimmed with panels of billboard size
depicting clouds and sky in unmistakable

hues of bluish twilight, that advertise
with enormous, printed slogans: *The Art
of Waterside Living,* and *Living in a Masterpiece.*

That uncanny shudder, a nervous start—
almost as though his ghost was summoned,
in the form of his *Nocturnes*, to distort

the genius of his paintings' ample vision
of city, river, sky in full embrace—
here branded as a commercial version.

Back at the river, the heron stays,
still as an obelisk. I walk with the rising tide
toward Chelsea Embankment, keeping pace

with the water, passing neighborhoods gentrified
in Whistler's time, and passing several houses
where Whistler lived; the one in which he died.

Beside me, the Embankment wall composes
a gallery of lichens—a "harmony,"
as Whistler might have called their flattened roses

of sage and mustard. Or, more aesthetically,
perhaps he'd name their hues *gray-green and gold;*
not that it matters what Whistler'd say. . . .

They seem mere splatters, but are really very old,
and grow by silent, slow collaboration,
a symbiosis of bacteria and mold:

if beautiful, then beauty in the margins,
like birds in that waste space, mouth of the canal.
They advertise—in the sense of "turn attention"—

their mere presence, immediate, on this wall.
An affinity here. "Art," wrote Whistler, "happens."
As, perhaps, the *Nocturnes* happen to reveal

unintended presences that haunt the seams
of urban & urbane intent. . . . A moorhen, a dozing heron—
they tilt the city, slightly, from its frame.

A Found Piece

Whistler, writing from Corsica, 1901

". . . sudden, you know, it struck me
I had never
rested, never done

nothing, nothing was the one thing
I needed!
And I put myself down

to doing
nothing—amazing,
you know, no more

sketch-books—no more
plates. Just sat
in the sun and . . .

cured. . . ."

IV.

Ars Longa Which is crueler
Vita Brevis life or art?
  —ROBERT HAYDEN, "THE PEACOCK ROOM"

I have kept her house—in its freshness and rare beauty
as she had made it—and, from time to time,
I go to miss her in it—
  —JAMES McNEILL WHISTLER

View from a Canal Street Hotel

In this tenth-floor view of the city,
all the work wrought through centuries
is distanced to panorama. Glinting
in sunlight, it feels like a gift: a "view,"
a single thing that, including all, includes
me, in a comfortable kind
of anonymity.

           Not like that name
I saw yesterday, engraved in gilded
roman letters, outside the entrance
to the Metropolitan Museum.
It's not that I'm not used to seeing
wealthy names mounted on the side
of buildings. I enjoy my share
in the largesse of patrons, and I'd be a liar
to say I mind their giving.
But this billionaire also pays—handsomely—
to muddle to his own advantage
the discourse of our democracy.
He gives *that* money anonymously.
I don't think it's modesty.
Rather, I suppose, a strategy
for greed to stay, like a gilded frame,
out of the picture.

           —But what's that thing
clinging to a building over there
like a giant woodpecker,
or a tiny King Kong?
Squinting, I can make it out:
a window washer—leaning back
into the harness belt, feet braced
on the sill, his center of gravity suspending
over hundreds of feet of nothing

between him and rooftops, water tanks,
awnings, trucks, people on sidewalks:
how he depends,
in the radical sense of the word,
on two metal hooks
and an implicit trust in the work
of someone he doesn't know
who, decades ago,
had anchored those hooks.

                            I love
his focus, his movements'
angular, efficient precision—truly
what we mean when we say "clean."
When he finishes, and clambers back
inside the window, I still scan
the building, hoping he'll reappear.
When it hits me: how clearly I see
he's gone—that is, the window
I'm looking through all this time
is *clean*. I've been gazing right through
some window washer's work,
someone both worthy and
anonymous, like the ancient artists
of Egypt, Greece, and Rome
whose work bears quiet witness
on the museum's ground floor.

An Exhibit of Audubon's Paintings

My friend trained in painting and drawing
who makes a living making maps, observes
how these shorebirds, shown in profile, set
on mud or rock, might open a window
on a time when things were seen
as objects, and understood that way: a thing
among other things. A bittern among reeds.

Which seems only obvious, at first,
till I wonder, what was it like when,
some fifty years later, James McNeill Whistler,
seeing watery twilight sky reflected on water,
thought, *I want to paint that;* and meant by *that*
a luminous movement, what we call,
because we insist on nouns, *light* and *time.*

I'd thought of Whistler last night—
when rooftops were backlit with a rose-gray sky
inset with blue-silver medallions of cloud. . . .
I don't know that Whistler ever painted a bird
(aside from a couple of allegorical, gold-leaf peacocks)
but he painted waves, and evening.
                                        The sky
in Audubon's paintings, when there is one, is token—
a cliché cloud, likely painted by an assistant;
an object to designate "sky," a reference point
to situate a bittern firmly on the ground.
If dark clouds loom, it's to enclose some white
bird in its whiteness—pelican, gannet, snowy owl.

Still, there's no doubt how Audubon
loved these birds. He would paint them alive,
when possible. Maps of Florida and Labrador
mounted on the walls trace his travels
to seek them in their habitats;
while even now, he's drawn us in
to the landscape of the frigate bird's back
by giving each barb of each feather its own
glossy stroke of the pencil.

At last, when we think we're done with looking,
we leave, and wander Central Park,
walking paths we haven't walked
in decades. It's early May, a Whistler sky
of rain clouds dissolving into light suspends
above trees and gardens punctuated
with migrant birds—close in, the redstart,
yellowthroat, and ovenbird delineate themselves
unmistakably; and others, higher up,
I can't name. In the rivery
motion and breadth of park and city and weather,
our eyes range from catbird to atmosphere,
stirring a slowly welling thrill, as our talk
wings back and forth between us.

Ultrasound

It reminds me of Whistler's etching of the forge—
in this: brightness where what is fashioning
dazzles against dark. He knew it needn't be large:
engravings, like gems, gain luster by compression.

But it's ultra*sound*—an instrument played upon
her body, pulsing in millionth-notes
that change in pitch when touching tissue, fluid, bone;
the echoes then transposed to waves of light.

Womb-music made visible, inked on paper—
still, only analogy. One could say it looks like an eye,
and the highlight in its pupil holds the shape
of a kidney bean,—or Australia. It prompts no lullaby.

Though graven with future: shadowed in this flimsy leaf,
my own knees buckling, in gratitude, or grief.

The Peacock Room

To me, at least, home means as much as my soul.
—STÉPHANE MALLARMÉ TO WHISTLER

I think of a room as an intended space,
its plan an extension of the mind;
which leads me to this room where I try
to write. The mess of it. Dogs. Shedding,
shredding, and the new one, shitting on the rug.
A trunk I bought on Canal Street
nearly forty years ago, and lugged ever since.
My baggage itself a kind of baggage.

If rooms are intentions ("Let's go in the living room,
and live," said Groucho), then the rooms I live in
don't so much comprise as compromise
between a wished-for self, and the real:
the simplicity of my study,
and the frenzied still-life of its clutter.
And the midden of wasted paper,
half-scrawled and abandoned, on the desk.
I call it a study, but it's really a dining nook,
repurposed. We don't "dine."

Imagine a dining room designed
expressly to display your porcelain. Or imagine
you *have* a porcelain collection fine enough
to provide the decor for your dining room designed
to display it. Imagine a room so exquisite
it's twice been disassembled and moved—
and now is a room on the map of a museum,
enshrined on the National Mall in D.C.
Imagine the Peacock Room.

Sitting in the Peacock Room, among Chinese vases
arranged on a lattice of gilded shelves,
panels of leather painted blue, filigreed
with gold leaf in peacock feather motif,
I am of three minds. My self—that lamprey
of consciousness. Frederick Leyland, self-made
magnate, owner of ships. And James McNeill Whistler,
artist advertised by his monocle.
I suppose, too, there's the dog.

Leyland held a shooting party at his named estate;
among the guests was Whistler, who shot
one of the hounds by mistake.
The dog was caught in a crossfire of pride:
Leyland's, that if you hire enough people to build
a house large enough, the house appears
as if it's *meant* to be, and meant for *you;*
then Whistler's, son of a West Point man, and he too
a West Point man (till he was kicked out),
assuming an officer's panache with a gun.

Intention: to shoot a pheasant. To marry.
To command a place at the patron's table.
To compose oneself within the lines of poems,
or rooms. To abide within a stanza,

a marriage bed. To pull the trigger;
but not to wound the dog. Intention:
two years building the child's wooden dollhouse.
What sort of intention, to shove it to the floor?

Intention: to pull the trigger, but not become
the trigger. Repeat the words to echo in a poem;
not words meant to rhyme the pain
of their first utterance. The peacock's sheen,

without the shriek. The utter non-intention
of the radio playing that piece by Fauré
we chose for our wedding. Sweet order
of music, roiling in my room.

Strip down the peacock and it's just another
lizardly fowl. Strip the Peacock Room's plumage,
the gold leaf and blue paint, and find
panels of antique Spanish leather—
cowhide overlaid in silver leaf, ambered
with shellac till it looks like gold.

This honeyed, translucent sunrise scheme
was conceived in the brain of one
Thomas Jeckyll, the room's first designer,
ingenious at patterns, though unsteady
of mind. When Jeckyll's prepossession left him
unmoored, Whistler was called in to finish.

Who first confined himself to refinements
of Jeckyll's gold and brown design.
But then, the walnut shelving seemed too dark;
so Whistler took to gilding, then finessed the tone
of the painted primrose pattern. . . .
(And the dog: What are these teeth that bite me?)

It's 5 a.m. and my mind, searching, scans
the windows, panes dark as onyx, reflecting
a pallid, backward version of my room.
At 2:38, my wife's last text, sent
where she struggled to sleep behind the wall
of another room in the same house. Unjust

love, that, baffled, cuts us down. Unjust
and true, in the heart's tautology:
that what you feel is what you feel.
Earlier I left the house—I won't say
"our" house—to get away from our shared
screams, and blame, the chiasmus of pointless
argument: screams of blame and blame for screams.
A few beers and a basketball game
on the local bar's TV. And then back "home."
Where I do not go gentle, cannot go goodnight.

This ambiguous space I call my "study"
(half-passageway between kitchen and living room),
and a gesture by my wife I don't know how to read—
white doily of baking soda on the rug,
spread there to absorb the dogshit smell.
All I have wanted was to love, love well,
and be loved. And to be honest: at times
to be left alone. As I tried to slam the door
it struck our dog who'd bounded over, expecting
his usual walk. His, the last cry.

Still, the room needed something. Not in the way
that Leyland needed steamships, a means
to an end, the end being, always for the merchant,
profit. For Whistler, it was the unaccountable
need that produces, as nature produced,
unaccountably, the peacock.
So let there be, as Whistler said
in a press release, "A pattern invented
from the eye of the peacock," and "a pattern derived
from the breast feathers." Let them emanate
and multiply, in fugue-like unfurling,
until all that Spanish leather is swallowed
in a vision of gold leaf and Prussian blue.

The room becomes an event—Princess Louise,
and the Marquess of Westminster, even Prince Edward
pay visits to the fledging space; they
"keep up the buzz of publicity
most pleasantly in London Society."
Whistler bids the servants to furnish
tea and luncheon; now hosts an invited
gathering of the press; now an evening concert,
The Peacock Room listed on the program.

One visitor was Thomas Jeckyll, newly
composed, come to see the progress
of his design. It's said they found him later,
on his knees, gilding the floor of his apartment.

I too have painted a room—
the living room my study opens onto. Living
so much in my mind, my mind
needs to look outward, away from itself,

so I placed my chair to face
the living room, an upholstered
vista, with a glimpse (in daylight)
of the park beyond. . . .

Still, the room needed something.
Weeks to choose the color, in satin finish,
that walls may seem to breathe with light.
And the trim, the difficult white,

with faintest wisp, subliminal hint, of blue.
The family driven from the room,
domestic exile of sandpaper and caulk,
rolled up rug and sawdust, tape, tarp:

as if somehow that painterly prospect—
a park framed by a living room framed
by a study—were a metaphor
of blended art and life.

Whistler submits a bill for the room: two thousand
guineas. Leyland pays him one thousand
pounds. The difference is more than half the sum:
a guinea is a pound plus a shilling—
a kind of gratuity, a mark of respect.
Which Leyland's saying Whistler doesn't deserve.

So Whistler declares he'll pay himself
with his own art. As if a whole economy—investor,
producer, consumer—were contained in his brush.
Like Rumpelstiltskin, he spins gold. Not from straw,
but with hog bristles tipped with gold leaf, he spins
peacock eyes and the scales of its breast.

On the wall facing where the master,
Leyland, will preside at dinner, an allegory:
two peacocks in combat, one with ruffled neck
like the frilled shirts Leyland wore that hoards
a pile of silver coin; the other, with white plume
like the single white lock in Whistler's hair,

stands its ground, unruffled.
Where's my Spanish leather? Leyland demands.
He's just returned from Liverpool, and caught
Whistler roosting on a ladder, fanning
a paintbrush. *Your Spanish leather,* says Whistler,
is right here, beneath my beautiful peacocks.

Plotinus wrote that art descends to us
from a godly realm—a thought like a breeze, unseen
but felt, wafting from divine to human mind;
that so informed, the artist then can look
right *through* the marble block,
and liberate the form that's lodged within.

You can bet Plotinus never held a chisel.
No beard and eyebrows talced with marble dust,
turning to plaster in the lungs.
Did Plotinus ever price a block of marble?
Did his rent depend on selling a portrait?
And what about the family dog: who feeds it?

The Peacock Room disassembled, twice moved—
to another mansion, then this museum
where I slouch on a hard bench placed
where Leyland's table would have stood.

Gallery-weary, I have become
another fixture tourists move among.
Funny, but spending time
in the Peacock Room, I've learned

I don't much like the Peacock Room.
There's no respite from its gold and blue;
the countless strokes of feathers speak insistently
of effort, mere effort. Impressive

for effort alone—the only grandeur
of this hard-won failure.
I know when I return home,
we will sell the house, empty

the rooms. The rooms will stay,
get painted over. We'll go.
Sitting in the Peacock Room,
all the pain within this paint,

I need to believe
it is the same with love;
that, all grace worn down,
there still lives, if only by force

of effort—effort intended
by love—some shape that resists
erasure. I know no name for it. Not
beauty. But also, not its opposite.

CODA

We'll build in sonnets pretty rooms
—JOHN DONNE

"Jehovah holds the hand with which I draw,"
    writes Jeckyll from the asylum where he's gone
        since returning to the room, wherein he saw
            the remnants of his vision. Which were none.
I'm sitting in my study, close to dawn,
    surrounded by a ghostly family
        of shadows, lovely for a while, but shown,
            in graying light, to be a fantasy.
There's Leyland blustering: "I will publicly
    horsewhip" the man he calls "artistic Barnum."
        And Whistler: "Once a friend, always an enemy!"
            condemning Leyland with no chance of pardon.
Whistler never sees the Peacock Room again.
The dog survives, and soon begins to mend.

The Lamp

Little Rose of Lyme Regis, The Siesta

It's November, 1895. To his wife who will die
before summer, James Whistler writes "a word or two
of hope." He's in a coastal village in Dorset
where he's gone to paint—she urged him to,
knowing that immersion in his work is all
that can ease his mind from the effort of denying
what will surely happen. In the village of Lyme Regis,
he's painted a blacksmith and a young girl.
In his letter to his wife, among gossip and unreal plans
for travel to America together, he writes about "the Lamp."

The Lamp is part of their private language,
like the pet names and the jokes. Like Aladdin's,
the Lamp holds rewards; but only suffering, it seems,
can rub them into being. The Lamp has to do with time,
by which work will be (this is my word) *accomplished.*
She knows this. But there is one moment
when he writes to her of something new, and urgent,
about "the real light of *untiring love,*
and purity, which finally become knowledge."

I think he was pointing to this, when he wrote,
"Especially look at the head of little Rosie,"
his portrait of Rosie Randall, the mayor's daughter.
Perhaps only a child could meet his gaze
so full on, so openly—(even the master blacksmith
folds his arms across his chest, looks at the painter
sideways, holding his strength to himself)—because,
eight years old, she has become a person,
and she knows this; but cannot fully fathom her life
yet unlived: for she is at once "Rose," and "little."
But it's also the way he meets *her* gaze. I can't tell
if the joy he feels is more from having seen so well,
or the skill of his hand in painting her.

Later that winter, he is drawing his wife at rest,
cervical cancer having leeched her strength away.
In this process, he draws with a wax pencil
on transfer paper, which he will later press
onto polished stone. The stone will keep the image
long enough to reproduce. In *The Siesta*
(as though it were only that), a few lines
to capture the bed, the comforter. Her forearm,
drawn pencil-thin, droops from her sleeve;
her fingers, limp shadows, a counterweight
to the focal point: the dark tones
and highlights of her hair, the oval of her face,
white as paper, and within, her eyes
looking back at him, with brows raised
to open them slightly more, in a soft question
answered by the touch of pencil tip to paper.
At last, he brings his art to bear on love.
"Not the slightest flaw," his printer said,
when the image was transferred to stone.

Sitting in November

I must sit *hard* and not think—
—WHISTLER

November now, it's come to this, my morning
routine: to sit on the bedroom floor
before the tall window, legs half-lotused
like a monk, in underwear, and stare.
I'm looking at nothing but weather that,
rhyming with "whatever," serves not
so much as emblem, but example of all
that just happens, unbidden, each day.

Briefly, we waited for another child. It grew
inside her some twelve weeks, unfurling
like a leaf, and about that size, until the cord
withered like—yes, I'll say it—a November stem.
That was August. And since then, further grief
has grown around us, like cancer. *As* cancer:
no simile. Our longest friend,
who gave us (like a mother) porcelain
for our wedding, who shared meals and wine
and talk of books in her own home,
has now withdrawn; as if to say her dying
is hers, but ours alone
the mourning we've already begun.

Sunlight strikes the lingering oak leaves
so that they glow like plums.
By afternoon, a wind-driven wall of dust
could brown out the sun:
here on these page-flat plains,
where what blows in is passively received,
November weather could be anything.
The trick, of course, is to resist the urge
to read a meaning in.

My mother had nine children, loved each one
completely. What fullness, split nine ways,
stays full? I was the ninth child, and believed,
until my twenties, that I was the last.
Then she mentioned she'd been pregnant
after me—which resurrected a memory,
the memory itself some fifty years old:
our living room, I'm on the rug, crawling;
my mother is seated on a couch between
my father and the priest. I don't know
that he's a priest, this stranger in black,
with a white collar. I don't know anything
except for this: my mother begins to weep,
and no one can comfort her. And what can I do,
if *she* is crying, but cry, and louder,
until someone's hands are lifting me up
to carry me from the room?

That was the moment I entered time.
Echoed now, in our womb-lost child.
And all I've learned in fifty years
is no amount of love will let you keep
your loved ones. My mother's grief,
charged as her ninefold love, couldn't hold
that child; and when she, too, died,
we five brothers buckled with sobs,
carrying her coffin's all-too-bearable weight.
One could be philosophical, and choose
to love what doesn't change,
though it's likely that turns out to be
the constancy of change. Or else
there's "Offer it up," as my mother would say,
offering us the enlargement of sacrifice,
to imitate the suffering of Christ, or God,
"Who gave His only Son"—as if a god
from whom nothing can be removed
could really lose at all.

I may as well just sit here, cross-
legged on the sun-warmed floor,
look out the window, and try not to think;
or thinking, try not to mean. Unless
there might be consolation in philosophy
misunderstood. I'm thinking of the story
Plato put in Aristophanes's mouth,
of the origin of love: how humans once
were four legs, four hands, two faces merged
in a single person. But maybe it wasn't soul
and soul's beloved, joined in one body,
that had been sundered by the gods,
leaving each soul to scramble for its mate.
Maybe it was the soul and the soul's own
personal, chosen and given, character
of grief. This could almost make sense—as much
as anything else I've got: that we spend
our days in search of our perfect
sorrow, suspecting that love's
the likeliest place it would hide.

NOTES

This book reflects on the life and art of James Abbott McNeill Whistler (1834–1903), American expatriate painter. The title is taken from Whistler's collection of correspondence, reviews and commentary titled *The Gentle Art of Making Enemies,* first published in 1890.

DOMESTIC NOCTURNE: "his grown son" is Charles James Whistler Hanson (1870–1935). Born to Louisa Hanson, a parlormaid, raised by Joanna Hiffernan, model for and mistress of Whistler. Other children of Whistler's were, as the poem states, put up for fostering or adoption and not acknowledged by Whistler.

PORTRAIT IN FRAGMENTS: Whistler, the son of a military engineer, attended the United States Military Academy at West Point but was discharged for failing his academic studies. He ranked first, however, in drawing. The Superintendent of West Point at the time was Robert E. Lee.

   Maud Franklin was a model and mistress for Whistler, and a painter in her own right. She bore at least two children by Whistler.

WIG LADY: For the residents of 60 W. 14th St., in the day.

ROTHERHITHE: In part V, "Benjamin" is the German critic, Walter Benjamin (1892–1940).

LETTER TO WHISTLER: "Billet à Whistler," by Stéphane Mallarmé, written in 1890. Mallarmé's sonnet was prompted by a design Whistler drew for the arts journal, *The Whirlwind.* Many poets have written in response to Whistler's art, beginning in 1865, when Swinburne wrote "Before the Mirror" for Whistler's *Symphony in White, No. 2: The Little White Girl.*

THE ARTIST IS REBORN: The "single lecture, presented at ten o'clock of a Friday," refers to Whistler's public lecture, "Ten O'Clock," in which he presented his aesthetics of painting before an audience of the London *beau monde.*

The italicized lines are from the first biography of Whistler, *The Life of James McNeill Whistler* by Elizabeth Robins Pennell and Joseph Pennell, first published in 1908.

THE TRIAL: In 1878 Whistler sued the prominent critic, John Ruskin, because of Ruskin's review of Whistler's *Nocturne in Black and Gold: The Falling Rocket*. Ruskin accused Whistler of "cockney impudence," writing that he "never expected to hear a coxcomb ask two hundred guineas for flinging a pot of paint in the public's face." Considering the statement damaging to his career as a painter, Whistler sued for libel.

Quotations in the poem are largely taken from the transcript of the trial. However, since the participants did not speak in ottava rima stanzas (though often iambically), I have reluctantly rephrased them as needed.

BANKRUPT: Whistler won his lawsuit against John Ruskin, but was awarded only one farthing in damages: a sign that the court considered his case frivolous. The legal expenses tipped his precarious finances into bankruptcy.

THE CITY: The poem referred to is "The City" by Constantine Cavafy; the quoted line is from Lawrence Durrell's translation, printed in the "Notes" to his novel, *Justine*.

A FOUND PIECE: The text is derived, with slight adjustments, from Whistler's letter to Elizabeth Robins Pennell, written sometime in late winter or early spring of 1901.

THE PEACOCK ROOM: The formal dining room of the London home of Frederick Leyland, a shipping magnate and Whistler's patron in the 1870s. Hired to finish the work of designer Thomas Jeckyll, Whistler eventually transformed the room with his own design, which he titled *Harmony in Blue and Gold*. The room was later dismantled and moved to the home of Charles Lang Freer, in Detroit, and is now installed in the Freer Gallery of Art in the Smithsonian.

THE LAMP: Whistler married Beatrice Godwin in 1888. She died of ovarian cancer in 1896.

ACKNOWLEDGMENTS

Grateful acknowledgment is made to the editors of the following publications, in which some of these poems first appeared, sometimes in a slightly different form: *A Poetry Congeries:* "*Annie Seated*"; *Bellingham Review:* "Bankrupt"; *The Common:* "Domestic Nocturne"; *Georgia Review:* "Sitting in November" and "The Trial"; *Gettysburg Review:* "The Artist Is Born in Lowell"; *Hampden-Sydney Poetry Review:* "Sonnet"; *Harvard Review:* "An Exhibit of Audubon's Paintings"; *Literary Matters:* "The Chelsea Girl," "Letter to Whistler," and "The Artist Is Reborn"; *Raritan:* "Tending: A Nocturne"; *Sewanee Review:* "Living in a Masterpiece"; *Shenandoah:* "Whistler Paints a Portrait"; *Southern Review:* "Thames Music," "Portrait in Fragments," and "View from a Canal Street Hotel"; *Tar River Poetry:* "Two Lonelinesses"; *Terrain.org:* "Rotherhithe"; and *Threepenny Review:* "Wig Lady."

When the poem "Acknowledgments" mentions that Marcel Proust stole a glove from Whistler, it relays a fact I drew from Daniel E. Sutherland's biography of Whistler. Sutherland in turn attributes this item to William C. Carter's biography of Proust. Let this example illustrate by metonymy the web of indebtedness I owe to the scholarly and narrative skills of biographers; especially, for me: Elizabeth Robins Pennell and Joseph Pennell; Gordon H. Fleming; Ronald Anderson and Anne Koval; Linda Merrill; Daniel Sutherland. This book is not biography, and these poems make little distinction between historical and invented detail. All departures from fact are wholly my responsibility.

 I am grateful to Texas Tech University for grants that supported the research and writing of this book. I also acknowledge the University of Glasgow, which hosts the invaluable online edition of *The Correspondence of James McNeill Whistler, 1855–1903,* edited by Margaret F. MacDonald, Patricia de Montfort, and Nigel Thorp; including *The Correspondence of Anna McNeill Whistler, 1829–1880,* edited by Georgia Toutziari, http://www.whistler.arts.gla.ac.uk/correspondence.

For all their flaws, these poems are better than they would have been thanks to the attentions of Bruce Beasley, Robert Cording, Jeffrey Harrison, Jacqueline Kolosov, Suzanne Paola, and Daniel Tobin; which is to say, six times over, "the knowledge gained . . . in the work of a lifetime."

Printed in the USA
CPSIA information can be obtained
at www.ICGtesting.com
LVHW041040231023
761874LV00006B/234

9 780807 178713